NATURE WE NEED

T0008950

Why Do We Need BATS?

by Laura K. Murray

PEBBLE
a capstone imprint

Published by Pebble, an imprint of Capstone
1710 Roe Crest Drive, North Mankato, Minnesota 56003
capstonepub.com

Library of Congress Cataloging-in-Publication Data is available on the Library of Congress website.

ISBN: 9780756575113 (hardcover)
ISBN: 9780756575069 (paperback)
ISBN: 9780756575076 (ebook PDF)

Summary: Does the spooky image of a bat scare you? These unusual mammals are good for much more than a fright. Bats help pollinate plants. They help keep pests away from crops. And the echolocation they use to find their way around has taught us a lot about navigation.

Editorial Credits
Editor: Ericka Smith; Designer: Kayla Rossow; Media Researcher: Svetlana Zhurkin; Production Specialist: Katy LaVigne

Image Credits
Alamy: Bill Coster, 7, blickwinkel, 24; Associated Press: Imaginechina, 21; Dreamstime: Dan Rieck, 12, William Wise, 25; Getty Images: corbac40, 13, derwood05, 29 (bottom), Joe McDonald, 8, 23, Johner Images, 26, Keith Rose, 16, nymphoenix, 17, Oxford Scientific, 10, Subrahmanyan Puthiyillam, 15; Shutterstock: David Havel, 14, Faith Forrest (dotted background), cover and throughout, Fred Crema, 5, Lims java, 22, Maksim Shmeljov, 20, Maurizio Callari, 29 (top), Milan Zygmunt, 29 (middle), MilletStudio, 9, NataLT (leather background), cover, back cover, and throughout, oticki, 18, Pedro Luna, 19, Photoongraphy, 4, prasanthdaskkm, cover, Rob Jansen, 28, Rudmer Zwerver, 6, Sirisak Baokaew, 27; Superstock: Biosphoto/ Daniel Heuclin, 11

Table of Contents

Words in **bold** are in the glossary.

Night Flyers

Hundreds of bats hang inside a cave. At **dusk**, they fly out. They swoop through the dark. They catch a meal of insects.

Bats are often misunderstood. Some people think they are pests. Others think they are scary. But bats are an important part of nature. Humans, animals, and plants need them.

All About Bats

Bats are **mammals**. Their bodies are covered with hair. They are the only mammal that flies.

a golden-crowned flying fox

There are more than 1,400 kinds of bats. They come in all sizes. The smallest bat is a Kitti's hog-nosed bat. It weighs 2 grams. That's lighter than a penny! Its wingspan is about 6 inches (15.2 centimeters).

Flying foxes are the largest bats. The golden-crowned flying fox's wingspan is over 5 feet (1.5 meters)! And it weighs nearly 3 pounds (1.4 kilograms).

Bats live in most parts of the world.
Some bats that live in cold places
move to warmer areas in the winter.
Others **hibernate**. They store up fat.
It helps them stay alive.

bats hibernating

a bat colony

Bats live in all kinds of places. Some live in caves, trees, and rocky cliffs. Others make old mines and bridges their home. Some bats live in **colonies**. Others live alone.

Bats usually live up to 20 years. But some live more than 30 years!

Most bats are **nocturnal**. They are active at night. That's when they look for food.

Most bats eat insects. Some bats can eat more than 3,000 insects in one night! Other bats eat fruit, **nectar**, or **pollen**.

A vampire bat feeds on a goat.

The vampire bat has a strange diet. It drinks blood. It feeds on animals like cows and horses. Often the animals do not notice.

Sometimes bats bite humans. But it doesn't happen often.

Bats have special skills to catch their prey. They are great fliers! Their wings help them fly quickly and smoothly. The Brazilian free-tailed bat can fly up to 100 miles (161 kilometers) per hour.

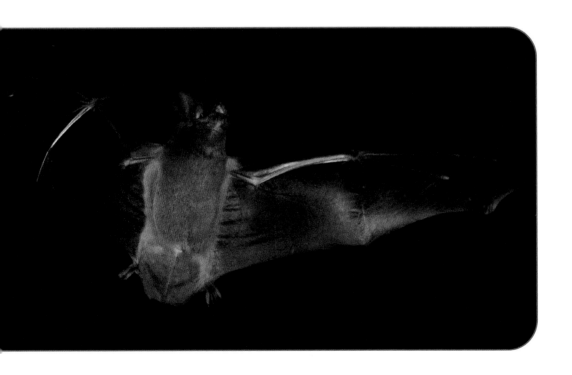

echolocation

Bats also use sound to hunt. This is called **echolocation**. A bat makes a sound. The sound waves bounce off objects. They come back to the bat's ears. The bat can tell where the object is. It can tell its size and shape too.

How Do Bats Help Us?

Bats help grow the food people eat. They are pollinators. They move pollen from one part of a flower to another. This helps plants grow seeds, fruits, or nuts.

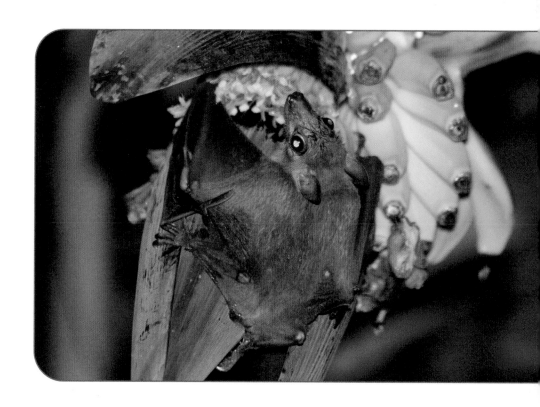

Many bats drink nectar from flowers. Their bodies pick up pollen as they drink. Then they move to another flower. They spread the pollen as they move.

Bats pollinate more than 300 kinds of plants. They help plants like bananas and peaches grow.

Some bats help plants and trees grow by spreading their seeds. The bats eat fruit from trees and plants. The seeds come out in their poop. This way, bats spread seeds far and wide.

Bats also help plants by controlling pests. Insects destroy crops. But bats eat lots of insects. This helps protect crops.

Farmers save money because of bats' help. They don't have to use as many **pesticides**. In 2011, bats saved farmers in the United States around $3 billion.

People also use guano—dried bat poop—to grow plants. It has nutrients. It helps protect plants from **fungi** and some pests.

Other animals need bats too. In caves, bat poop is food for animals like crickets and mites. Bats are also prey. Animals like hawks and owls eat them.

a cave cricket

People learn from bats' behavior. They study how bats use echolocation. People use sonar and radar in the same way. Sonar shows things underwater. Radar shows things in the air.

radar technology

People study bats' bodies too.
It helps them make things like drones.
They even study vampire bat spit for
use in medicine.

Threats to Bats

People are one threat to bats They might feel scared and kill them. Sometimes they destroy the places bats live and the food bats eat. They spray chemicals that harm bats. And wind farms can be dangerous for bats.

People can also harm bats by disturbing them during hibernation. The bats become active too early. They can use up their stored fat and starve.

Disease is a big threat to bats. They can get white-nose syndrome. A white fungus grows on hibernating bats. It makes them too active, and they burn the fat they need to survive. The disease spreads quickly too. It can kill a whole colony.

a bat with white-nose syndrome

a bat active during the day that might have rabies

Bats are known for carrying **rabies**. But less than one percent of bats have rabies. Bats with rabies do strange things like flying during the day. To stay safe, people should not touch bats.

A World Without Bats

Can you imagine a world without bats? Many plants and animals would die. There would be no chocolate or bananas. Cacti would not grow.

Insects would be a huge problem. Illnesses spread by insects would be more common. Farmers would use more pesticides.

Bats are amazing creatures. From eating insects to spreading seeds, they have important roles in nature. People, animals, and plants depend on bats. They're a part of nature we need!

COOL FACTS ABOUT BATS

• Bat wings have four fingers and a thumb, just like a human hand!

• Bats eat a lot of insects—and quick! A little brown bat can eat about 1,000 insects in one hour.

• Some bats stay clean by grooming one another.

• In Central America, the Honduran white bat shapes leaves into a tent to protect itself from rain.

• Texas's Bracken Cave is home to the world's largest bat colony. It's home to more than 15 million Mexican free-tailed bats.

Glossary

colony (KAH-luh-nee)—a group of one kind of animal

dusk (DUHSK)—the time of day after sunset when it is almost dark

echolocation (eh-koh-loh-KAY-shuhn)—the process of using sounds and echoes to locate objects

fungi (FUHN-jy)—organisms that have no leaves, flowers, or roots

hibernate (HYE-bur-nate)—to spend winter in a deep sleep

mammal (MAM-uhl)—a warm-blooded animal that breathes air; mammals have hair or fur; female mammals feed milk to their young

nectar (NEK-tur)—a sweet liquid in many flowers

nocturnal (nok-TUR-nuhl)—active at night and at rest during the day

pesticide (PES-tuh-side)—a poisonous chemical used to kill insects, rats, and fungi that can damage plants

pollen (POL-uhn)—tiny, usually yellow grains in flowers

rabies (RAY-beez)—a deadly disease that people and animals can get from the bite of an infected animal

Read More

Labrecque, Ellen. *Do Vampire Bats Really Drink Blood?: Answering Kids' Questions.* North Mankato, MN: Capstone, 2021.

Lopetz, Nicola. *Creepy but Cool Bloodsuckers.* New York: Crabtree, 2022.

Perish, Patrick. *Brown Bats.* Minneapolis: Bellwether Media, 2022.

Internet Sites

Britannica Kids: Bat
kids.britannica.com/kids/article/bat/352835

DK Find Out!: Bats
dkfindout.com/us/animals-and-nature/bats

National Geographic Kids: 10 Brilliant Bat Facts!
natgeokids.com/uk/discover/animals/general-animals/bat-facts

Index

About the Author

Laura K. Murray is the Minnesota-based author of more than 100 published or forthcoming books for young readers. She loves learning from fellow readers and helping others find their reading superpowers! Visit her at LauraKMurray.com.